My *State*
NORTH DAKOTA

By Christina Earley

TABLE OF CONTENTS

A Crabtree Seedlings Book

Crabtree Publishing
crabtreebooks.com

T0020353

School-to-Home Support for Caregivers and Teachers

This book helps children grow by letting them practice reading. Here are a few guiding questions to help the reader build his or her comprehension skills. Possible answers appear in red.

Before Reading:

• What do I know about North Dakota?
  • *I know that North Dakota is a state.*
  • *I know that North Dakota has plains.*

• What do I want to learn about North Dakota?
  • *I want to learn which famous people were born in North Dakota.*
  • *I want to learn what the state flag looks like.*

During Reading:

• What have I learned so far?
  • *I have learned that Bismarck is the state capital of North Dakota.*
  • *I have learned that there are thousands of prairie dogs at Theodore Roosevelt National Park.*

• I wonder why…
  • *I wonder why the state flower is the wild prairie rose.*
  • *I wonder why Minot has the largest Scandinavian festival in North America.*

After Reading:

• What did I learn about North Dakota?
  • *I have learned that New Salem has the largest cow sculpture in the world.*
  • *I have learned that the state bird is the western meadowlark.*

• Read the book again and look for the glossary words.
  • *I see the word **capital** on page 6, and the word **walleye** on page 17. The other glossary words are found on pages 22 and 23.*

2

3

I live in Minot. The Mouse River runs through my city.

My city has the largest **Scandinavian festival** in North America.

Bismarck

North Dakota is in the **midwestern** United States. The **capital** is Bismarck.

Fun Fact: Fargo is the largest city in North Dakota.

The state bird is the western meadowlark.

The wild prairie rose is the state flower.

9

Fun Fact: North Dakota is one of the states that grows the most wheat in the U.S.

My state flag is blue. It has a bald eagle in the middle.

New Salem has the largest cow sculpture in the world.

I go horseback riding with my family at Theodore Roosevelt National Park. Sometimes we see bison!

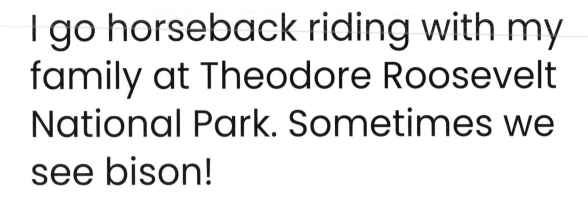

Fun Fact: There are thousands of prairie dogs at the park.

The Turtle Mountains are perfect for snowmobiling.

I try to catch **walleye** on Lake Sakakawea.

Cara Mund, who was Miss America in 2018, was born in North Dakota. Actor Josh Duhamel was also born in North Dakota.

Fun Fact: Former astronaut and lieutenant general James A. Abrahamson was born in Williston, North Dakota.

I like to explore the **earth lodge** at Knife River Indian Villages.

I enjoy walking around the International Peace Garden.

Glossary

capital (cap-ih-tuhl): The city or town where the government of a country, state, or province is located

earth lodge (erth loj): A Native American dwelling that is circular in shape and covered with earth, branches, and grass

festival (fes-tuh-vuhl): An event where people gather to celebrate something

midwestern (mid-west-urn): The northern central part of the United States

Scandinavian (skan-duh-nay-vee-uhn): Relating to a group of northern European countries that includes Denmark, Norway, and Sweden

walleye (waul-ahy): A type of fish that lives in fresh water and has large eyes

Index

Written by: Christina Earley
Designed and Illustrated by: Bobbie Houser
Series Development: James Earley
Proofreader: Melissa Boyce
Educational Consultant: Marie Lemke M.Ed.

About the Author

Christina Earley lives in sunny South Florida with her husband and son. She enjoys traveling around the United States and learning about different historical places. Her hobbies include hiking, yoga, and baking.

Photographs:
Alamy: AB Forces News Collection: p. 5, 22-23; INTERFOTO: p. 19
Shutterstock: ZakZeinert: cover; Anh Luu: p. 3; Kristin Murchie: p. 4; Volina: p. 6, 22-23; David Harmantas: p. 7; David Spates: p. 8; oksana2010: p. 9; Charles Lemar Brown: p. 10-11; Scorpp: p. 11; railway fx: p. 12; JWCohen: p. 13; Natalia Kuzmina: p. 14; ZakZeinert: p. 14-15; Body Stock: p. 16; Life Atlas Photography: p. 17, 23; lev radin: p. 18 left; Kathy Hutchins: p. 18 right; Traveller70: p. 20, 22; Jacob Boomsma: p. 21

Crabtree Publishing

crabtreebooks.com   800-387-7650
Copyright © 2024 Crabtree Publishing

Printed in the U.S.A./072023/CG20230214

Published in Canada
Crabtree Publishing
616 Welland Avenue
St. Catharines, Ontario
L2M 5V6

Published in the United States
Crabtree Publishing
347 Fifth Avenue
Suite 1402-145
New York, New York, 10016

Library and Archives Canada Cataloguing in Publication
Available at Library and Archives Canada

Library of Congress Cataloging-in-Publication Data
Available at the Library of Congress

Hardcover: 978-1-0398-0529-3
Paperback: 978-1-0398-0561-3
Ebook (pdf): 978-1-0398-0625-2
Epub: 978-1-0398-0593-4

My Earth & Space Science Library

Protecting Our Planet

Lisa J. Amstutz

Rourke
Educational Media

A Division of
Carson
Dellosa
Education

Before Reading: *Building Background Knowledge and Vocabulary*

Building background knowledge can help children process new information and build upon what they already know. Before reading a book, it is important to tap into what children already know about the topic. This will help them develop their vocabulary and increase their reading comprehension.

Questions and Activities to Build Background Knowledge:

1. Look at the front cover of the book and read the title. What do you think this book will be about?
2. What do you already know about this topic?
3. Take a book walk and skim the pages. Look at the table of contents, photographs, captions, and bold words. Did these text features give you any information or predictions about what you will read in this book?

Vocabulary: *Vocabulary Is Key to Reading Comprehension*

Use the following directions to prompt a conversation about each word.
- Read the vocabulary words.
- What comes to mind when you see each word?
- What do you think each word means?

Vocabulary Words:
- chemicals
- gases
- pollutes
- recycle

During Reading: *Reading for Meaning and Understanding*

To achieve deep comprehension of a book, children are encouraged to use close reading strategies. During reading, it is important to have children stop and make connections. These connections result in deeper analysis and understanding of a book.

Close Reading a Text

During reading, have children stop and talk about the following:
- Any confusing parts
- Any unknown words
- Text to text, text to self, text to world connections
- The main idea in each chapter or heading

Encourage children to use context clues to determine the meaning of any unknown words. These strategies will help children learn to analyze the text more thoroughly as they read.

When you are finished reading this book, turn to the last page for an **After Reading Activity**.